The Science of

Cryptocurrencies:

Understanding, Trading and Investing In Bitcoin, Ethereum, Litecoin, Emercoin, Auroracoin, and the Blockchain Revolution

by Quawsi Samuel

© 2018

1

Author's Biography

Quawsi Samuel is a proud and savvy investment portfolio manager and medical and financial Underwriter. After receiving a Bachelors of Science at Sunderland University, Quawsi now works for a medium sized financial company in the Caribbean Islands with an asset base of 1.5 Billion USD in which he engages in Medical, financial and economical risk assessment and at the same time manages his personal investment portfolio business. He aspires to be an internationally recognized author, motivational speaker on various topics such as goal setting and achievement, Investments , finances and risk assessment. Quawsi firmly believes that the future will be in desperate need of proper financial and economic education as a result of the globalized economy we now live in. In his spare time, he loves spending time with his lovely wife and family, enjoys technically analyzing the forex, stocks, cryptocurrencies, commodities and the futures market and takes pleasure in reading a well crafted book in a variety of different genres.

Thank You

I will like to start by saying a heartfelt "thank you" for choosing to make this huge investment in your future with **The Science of Cryptocurrencies.** I appreciate your business. I really hope this book exceeds your expectation as you begin or continue your journey investing in Cryptocurrencies.

If this book has impacted you in anyway. Feel free to leave an honest review at my Amazon review page at

http://www.amazon.com/gp/product-review/B078XSLXXL

After leaving your review feel free to contact me at quawsisamuel@gmail.com to receive a **special offer.**

<u>Bonus!</u>

Wouldn't it be nice to have essential information for investing in Cryptocurrencies, forex, commodities ,stocks and options for Free. Well now is your Chance !!

Enter into web browser-http://eepurl.com/dgGQ5v

Simply click the above link to obtain a free promotional item. I would also give you full exclusive access to our service which I give relevant information, tips and strategic notification on a variety of investments markets and concepts that will help boost your returns on investment.

Table of Contents

By reading this document, the reader agrees that under no circumstances is the author responsible for any losses, direct or indirect, which are incurred as a result of the use of information contained within this document, including, but not limited to, —errors, omissions, or inaccuracies.

Introduction

I would like to thank you for purchasing the book *"The Science of Cryptocurrencies: Understanding, trading and investing in Bitcoin, Ethereum, Litecoin, Emercoin, Auroracoin, and the Blockchain revolution."*

Not so long ago, the Internet was an alien concept. However, now it is virtually impossible to imagine life without the Internet. Likewise, cryptocurrency was a foreign concept until a decade ago. Digital currency has revolutionized the world of commerce. Bitcoin ushered in the age of digital currency that has the power of replacing the age-old system of fiat currencies.

Cryptocurrencies are radically different from the paper money standard that we make use of and are faster, cheaper, easier to use, and more democratic than any other monetary standard in existence at present. There are different types of cryptocurrencies in existence, and they all make use of a similar technology that is known as the blockchain technology.

In this book, you will learn about what cryptocurrencies are, their advantages, the risks they pose, and their various uses. You will also learn about the different types of cryptocurrencies in existence, tips for investing in them, and about blockchain technology. You can get a better understanding of the futuristic world of cryptocurrencies by making use of the information provided in this book.

Thank you once again for choosing this book, I hope you find it informative.

Chapter One: What Is Cryptocurrency?

A cryptocurrency is a digital currency, and it is a virtual medium of exchange. It makes use of cryptography for securing and verifying transactions and for controlling the formation of different units of a specific crypto. Cryptocurrencies are limited entries in a vast database that cannot be changed unless certain conditions are fulfilled. During the tech boom in the '90s, several attempts were made at creating digital currency by using systems like Flooz, DigiCash, and Beenz, but they all failed. There were different reasons for their failure like fraud, financial difficulties, and tiffs between the companies and their employees as well. All those systems made use of a trusted third-party approach, wherein the companies verified and facilitated the transactions.

The creation of a virtual currency system was a lost cause due to the failures of these companies. However, in the early bit of 2009, an anonymous programmer or group of programmers under the alias of Satoshi Nakamoto created the Bitcoin. The Bitcoin network was described by Satoshi as an electronic peer-to-peer cash system. It means the system was decentralized and there were no servers or central controlling authorities involved in its creation.

The concept of Bitcoins was quite similar to the peer-to-peer network used for sharing files. Every payment network has to overcome a significant problem, and that is the issue of double spending. Double spending is a fraudulent technique of spending the same amount twice. The conventional solution to this problem was the involvement of a third party or a central server who would verify the transactions and keep track of the balances. However, this method entrusts a third party or the central authority with the control of all your funds. When it comes to a decentralized network like the one used by Bitcoin, every single participant on the network has to be involved.

The public ledger that the blockchain network uses has a record of all the transactions that took place on the web, and everyone can view this record. Every participant in the system can see the account balance of all the others on the blockchain. Every file consists the address of the sender, the public key of the recipient, and the number of coins transferred. The transaction needs to be verified and signed off by the sender using their private key. All these things form part of the basic cryptography used.

Once the deal has been vetted and confirmed, it is posted on the network. The transaction can be confirmed on the network only by solving certain cryptographic puzzles and miners are responsible for solving these puzzles. They take certain transactions, check their legitimacy, and then spread these across the network. Once this is done, different notes on the network keep adding it to their respective databases.

Whenever the transaction is confirmed it becomes a permanent part of the network, it cannot be reversed, and the miner receives a reward along with transaction fees. The cryptocurrency network is based on the unconditional consensus of all the participants relating to the legitimacy of the transactions and the balances. If the nodes on the network don't agree on a single balance, the entire system will crumble. However, different rules are programmed into the network to prevent its breakdown. Strong cryptography ensures that the process of consensus keeping and hence the name cryptocurrencies. This, along with the other factors mentioned above, help in making the concept of third parties and blind trust obsolete.

Buying Goods

Initially, it was quite difficult to find a merchant who would accept payment in the form of cryptocurrencies. However, with the increase in their popularity, this situation has been rectified. There are plenty of online and offline merchants who have started accepting different forms of cryptocurrency for payments. Big online retailers like Overstock, Newegg to small local businesses, and restaurants are accepting cryptos. Bitcoins can now be made use of for paying bills, shopping and acquiring goods as well. Other forms of digital currencies aren't that widely accepted at present; however, all this about to change soon. Things are getting better for the world of cryptos. Apple has recently authorized different cryptos as an acceptable form of payment on their app store. Of course, the users of other forms of digitized currency always have the option of converting their crypto holding into Bitcoins. There are a couple of online marketplaces like OpenBazaar and Bitify that only accept cryptocurrencies as a form of payment.

Investments

Most people believe that digitized currencies are the latest and the hottest investment opportunity on the block. Well, they indeed aren't mistaken. There are stories of plenty of people who have become millionaires because of their crypto holdings and investments. The most popular crypto happens to be Bitcoins, and the value of Bitcoins has skyrocketed in 2017. In November 2017, a single Bitcoin was worth more than $7000, making it more expensive than an ounce of gold. The second most popular and valued cryptocurrency is Ethereum, and even it has demonstrated quite a leap in its value. The value of Ether increased by 2700% in 2017. The combined market cap of all the cryptocurrencies has increased by more than 10,000% since the mid-2013. However, it is essential that you realize that cryptocurrencies are high-risk investments. The market value of these assets fluctuates more than any other investment. Moreover, digitized currency is unregulated and decentralized. Therefore, there is a scope of them being outlawed and let us not forget the threat of hacking. However, after all, that is said and done, cryptocurrencies are an excellent form of investment. You will learn more about minimizing the risks and improving your scope of investment in the coming chapters.

Mining

The most important aspect of the network of cryptocurrency is the miners. Akin to trading, even mining is a form of investment. Miners help in bookkeeping of all the transactions for their concerned community. The computing power of miners helps in solving cryptographic puzzles for confirming a transaction and then recording the same on the blockchain. The blockchain is the public ledger consisting all the transactions that were ever transacted on the network. A fascinating thing about mining is that with the increase in competition, the level of difficulty increases as well. So, the more popular a specific crypto becomes, the number of miners increases, and this increases the complexity of the puzzles as well. In the past, you could mine by using your regular computer or a powerful laptop as well. However, these days, you need to have the industrial-grade hardware for making a profit from mining. Litecoins, Dogecoins, and Feathercoins are cost-effective for a beginner. You might not be aware of how a miner earns his profit. The computing power they accumulate improves their chances of solving different cryptographic puzzles. After the miner solves these puzzles, he will get a reward along with a transaction fee for doing the same.

Accepted as a method of payment

If you own a business or are looking for any potential customers, then allowing digitized currencies, as a means of payment is a good idea. The interest garnered by cryptocurrencies is steadily increasing, and this futuristic currency is here to stay. Along with interest, different media for acquiring cryptocurrencies is growing as well. Like any other form of currency, even cryptos can be effectively made use of for payments.

Legality

Cryptocurrencies are steadily becoming mainstream, and with the increase in their popularity, different law enforcement agencies and other regulatory authorities all over the world are trying to understand the concept of these coins and the way in which they fit into the conventional currency system within the legal framework. When the Bitcoin was introduced, it led to the creation of a new paradigm regarding the financial system. Digitized currencies are self-sufficient, are decentralized in nature, and they don't exist in a physical form. A lot of concerns were raised about the decentralized and anonymous nature of these currencies. As of now, the legal status of these currencies is still undecided.

Chapter Two: Pros and Cons of Cryptocurrency

Advantages of cryptocurrencies

Prevention of fraud

Cryptocurrencies are digital, and they cannot be counterfeited. Every transaction after it has been verified becomes a permanent part of the blockchain. Also, a transaction cannot be arbitrarily reversed by a sender, unlike the working of a credit card chargeback.

Scope for immediate settlement

Whenever you are purchasing real estate, there are several third parties involved in the transaction like lawyers, estate agents, notaries and so on. Not just that, there is scope for delays and the applicability of a transaction fee. Think of the blockchain as an extensive database of property rights. The contracts of cryptocurrencies are designed and enforced in such a way that they have made the need for third parties obsolete. You don't need a third-party to verify the transaction and transactions are settled almost immediately without any delays.

Lower fees applicable

There are no transaction fees applicable on the exchange of cryptocurrencies since the miners are always compensated for by the network in which they are mining. Most of the Bitcoin or crypto exchanges don't have any transaction fee. However, if you start making use of third-party services for transacting or even safekeeping of your funds, then a transaction fee might be applicable. Even if a fee is payable, it is quite nominal.

No Identity theft

Whenever you are giving your credit card to a seller, you are giving that seller or the merchant access to your credit line regardless of the amount that is involved in it. All credit cards operate on a pull mechanism. Whenever a store or a merchant initiates a payment, the respective funds are automatically pulled from your account. However, all cryptos make use of a push mechanism wherein the holder of the specific crypto needs to send the exact amount without having to provide any other information to the recipient.

Access to everyone

More than half of the population in the world has access to the Internet and mobile phones. However, they don't have access to the traditional systems of exchange. In such cases, cryptocurrencies come in handy. All you need is a good Internet connection and a mobile phone for trading in digital currency. Not just that, physical boundaries and barriers don't matter when it comes to trade in these currencies.

Decentralization of the network

Cryptocurrencies make use of a digital network of computers that are spread all over the world. All these computers help in managing the record of transactions and for keeping track of any trade made. There is no central authority or regulatory body, which controls all this. However, with digitized currencies, no regulatory authority can manage it. It means that no one is authorized to take your tokens away from you, once you have established your ownership over them. Most of the digital currencies make use of a peer-to-peer network wherein the users have control of the network.

You own it

At present, apart from cryptocurrencies, there is no other system of electronic cash wherein your account isn't owned by some other party. For instance, let us look at PayPal. If the company is of the opinion that a particular account is being misused, then it has the power to freeze all the assets of that concerned account. It can be done even without the consultation of the account holder. However, when it comes to cryptocurrencies, as long as the holder of the cryptos has the private key, no one can take the funds away from the account. Unless you lose the keys yourself, your digitized currency will stay with you.

Disadvantages of cryptocurrencies

Lack of security

There is no safety net or a fail-proof way of protecting your cryptocurrencies from human errors, technical glitches, or fraud. Even if you aren't making use of a third-party wallet or exchange for transacting, if you forget your private keys, there is no possible manner in which you can recover your tokens once again. If your coins are stolen or lost, there is no central authority to whom you can report to for the recovery of your cryptocurrencies.

Increased regulatory norms

There aren't any guidelines per se regarding the regulation of these digitized currencies, and even if there are any, all the rules are entirely benign. The value of this currency would diminish quite significantly if any stringent rules were introduced. It would be even more devastating if bans were imposed on these currencies.

Limited scaling

Before a transaction can be recorded in the public ledger, it needs to be verified. This process of verification limits the speed and the quantum of transactions that can be processed on the network. Thereby, this limits the usage of these currencies as well. The fiat currencies that we make use of can be used for acquiring anything that you want. However, when it comes to cryptocurrencies, their usage is still restricted. The number of uses they can be put to is limited. The digitized currency system will take a while before it is anywhere near replacing the conventional fiat currency system.

Chapter Three: Investing In Cryptocurrencies

Now that you know what cryptocurrencies are all about and the various benefits they offer, the next step is to start investing in them. Cryptocurrencies like Bitcoin and Ethereum are considered to be the hottest investments in the market at present. These crypto tokens have the potential of becoming a form of non-manipulatable currency. The advocates of cryptocurrency believe that they can replace the fiat currency system in the word. Holding onto Bitcoins means that you are holding onto a share in this venture.

If Bitcoins manage to replace the monetary reserves of the central banks or become the currency for international trades, then the value of Bitcoins will skyrocket to unimaginable prices. Buying and holding cryptos is a good bet and it is like a security of the more significant ecosystem. In the past, all the crypto investors have managed to become quite successful. The appreciation of the value of these digitized coins is ridiculously good.

The value of Bitcoin has increased over 25,000% since 2001 and while that of Ethereum increased by 2700%. The market cap of all the significant cryptocurrencies has increased beyond 10,000% since 2013. These figures are mind-boggling, aren't they? You might be worried that this volatility in the prices might just be a temporary boom. Well, that's not necessarily true. It is brilliant if you have already invested in these tokens in the past. However, you don't have to worry about it.

Now that you realize the potential of these digitized currencies, the next logical step is to start investing in them. In this chapter, you will learn about investing in cryptocurrencies. You shouldn't be under the false assumption that cryptocurrencies are just like other regular investments. The volatility exhibited by these investments is exponentially higher than that showcased by other assets. Cryptocurrencies are indeed high-risk and high-return investments.

Why invest in cryptocurrencies?

By now you would have understood the different benefits the digitized currencies offer. There are three main functional reasons why investing in cryptos is a good idea.

The first reason is the inevitable devaluation of the fiat currencies. You can hedge your net-worth against any such impending devaluation by investing in cryptocurrencies. The second reason is the social vision that led to the creation of these currencies - the creation of free and hard money. The third reason is that you like and understand the technology that supports these coins. However, there are a couple of wrong reasons for investing in cryptocurrencies as well. People tend to fall prey to all the hype that surrounds these digitized currencies. Some investors are investing in these coins because they are scared of missing out and therefore, they end up buying it when it is at its peak for making money without actually understanding what it is all about. That's a recipe for disaster, and you should abstain from doing it.

Building your portfolio

The first cryptocurrency that was created was Bitcoin, and up until late 2016, not many were aware of any other cryptocurrencies. If you want to invest in cryptos, then you should do so intelligently. If you were to invest in stocks, would you place all your funds on just one particular stock or would you think of diversifying? You obviously would want to expand. Well, the same rule applies whenever you are investing in cryptocurrencies as well. You need to understand that there are several types of cryptocurrencies and not just Bitcoins.

The other types of digitized currencies are referred to as altcoins, and they are usually used for keeping the GPUs of miners going or that was the general belief. Well, all that has certainly changed now. Bitcoin is still the most popular type of cryptocurrency and enjoys a dominant share in the market, but that's not the only coin on the block. If you are interested in investing in cryptocurrencies, then you should think about building a portfolio comprising of different currencies. You should never place all your eggs in the same basket. You need a well-balanced crypto portfolio. You can include several other coins like Ethereum, Litecoin, Dash, Monero, Ripple, Auroracoin, Emercoin, and other coins.

For determining the value of the available tokens, you should always check the market cap of the relevant economy. Market capitalization isn't the perfect metric, but it does help you in recognizing the value of cryptocurrencies. Another strategy that you can make use of for creating a balanced portfolio is to reflect on the top ten valuable types of cryptos and then include them within your portfolio. Take some time out and read about the different coins and see if their vision makes sense to you.

For instance, some coins concentrate on privacy like Dash, Zcash, and Monero. Coins like Ethereum and Ethereum classic concentrate on smart contracts whereas Litecoin and Dash focus on scaling payments. Some cryptocurrencies like Ripple or Nem seem to be less open and decentralized when compared to Bitcoins. The financial market has come alive with cryptocurrency, and by understanding what you are dealing with; you can earn a good return.

If you are interested in buying altcoins, then you should make sure that you aren't being blind and set some rules to distinguish the good from the bad investments. Good coins are the ones whose technical vision is transparent, have an active team working on its development, and have an enthusiastic community of users and followers. Bad coins are those that aren't transparent and have a community base that focuses on making a quick buck.

How to buy cryptocurrencies?

Until a couple of years ago, it was quite a challenge to buy cryptocurrencies. However, all that has changed now and there are plenty of options to choose from.

Exchange traded notes

Let us start by buying Bitcoins. It is perhaps the most natural part, especially if you are amongst those who would like to invest in Bitcoins without going through the trouble of storing them. If you are amongst such investors, then you can make use of different investment media like the XBT tracker, the Bitcoin investment trust on Second Markets, the Bitcoin ETI, and other similar vehicles. With the increase in the popularity of Bitcoins, the number of brokers and exchanges trying to set up a financial product based on Bitcoins is increasing as well. All these investments ideas share one similarity, and they enable investors to bet on the price of Bitcoins without actually buying any Bitcoins per se. Most of the ardent fans of cryptocurrency would be of the notion that doing this takes away from the whole purpose of digitized currencies. You can make use of different channels of investment, and if something does go wrong, you always have a certificate of proof for indemnifying yourself. However, at present, no such investment product is in existence, but efforts are being made for creating something of this sort.

Buying real Bitcoins

You should consider buying Bitcoins directly if you are interested in possessing Bitcoins or if you don't want to pay fees for investment products. There are different exchanges that you can make use of for buying Bitcoins from exchanges. For instance, if you are in Europe, you can make use of Bitcoin.de or Kraken, in the USA you can use Coinbase, BitFinex, BitStamp, or Gemini; in Asian markets, you can use OKCoin, BitFlyer, or BTCChina. Buying Bitcoins is a straightforward process. You merely have to set up an account with the exchange, go through the verification process and start funding your account based on the fiat currency that you are using. On some exchanges, you don't have to maintain funds in your account and can instead trade on it directly with the other users on the platform. The exchange that you decide to make use of will depend on your geographic location. It is better to use an exchange that's close to you, at least physically. The chances of getting your money back legally are high if the exchange is located in the same jurisdiction as your residence. In case there isn't an exchange in the country you are living in, then you should consider using the services of a famous exchange located in a stable country. Also, depending on the kind of cryptocurrency you want to buy, the type of exchange you use will change. Most of the significant cryptocurrency exchanges deal in Bitcoins. The quantum of your investment will depend on your income, your financial needs, your ability to shoulder risk, and the kind of return you want.

Buying other cryptocurrencies

There are several other altcoins that you can consider investing in. Most of the significant cryptocurrency exchanges like Kraken, Coinbase, BitStamp, and BitFinex, have started adding different altcoins like Ethereum, Litecoin, Monero, and Ripple to their list of cryptocurrencies. If you are interested in diversifying your portfolio, then consider investing in other altcoins. Most of the exchanges that deal with altcoins tend to have KYC norms that are less strict, mainly because they don't deal with fiat currencies. It is quite likely that you will need to acquire Bitcoins before you can think about purchasing other cryptocurrencies. The process of buying Bitcoins is quite similar to the manner in which a dominant currency like the dollar would work in the forex market. Like with any Bitcoin exchange, you should be quite careful while selecting an exchange for altcoins as well. Most of the favorite altcoin exchanges are based in Asia, and you should do plenty of research before choosing one.

Is there a good time to buy?

There is no hard and fast rule regarding the perfect time for buying cryptocurrencies. As a general rule of thumb, you should avoid purchasing digitized tokens when it is at the peak of a bubble or when it is crashing. Never try catching a falling knife. Buy cryptocurrencies when the price of the concerned crypto is stable. The key to making a thriving trade is to decide when the crypto is growing in value and when it is ready to crash. Well, you need to follow any news regarding the crypto you are dealing with and closely monitor its progress. For instance, many didn't think that it was a wise idea to invest in Ethereum or even Bitcoins a couple of years ago when they were valued quite low. However, their prices have increased exponentially within a short duration. There are two necessary things that you should keep in mind when you are trying to time your crypto purchase. The first thing is that you should never compare a crypto bubble to a conventional financial bubble. More than 10% of the change in price can be attributed to daily volatility and not a bubble. On the other hand, a 100% increase can be a bubble, but that might just be the start. The second thing that you should do is take some time and notice the market trends. Don't buy something just because there was a dip in its price. Instead, wait for a while and see if there is another dip. Don't let the fear of being left out take hold of you and instead work on keeping calm. Don't sell too early and don't buy too soon. After all, the monetary revolution has just started, and there is plenty of time for you.

Methods of investing

Wallets

Once you have acquired cryptocurrencies, the next step is to work on storing them. There are several options that you can make use of for storing your cryptocurrencies, depending on the level of risk you are willing to take up. A cryptocurrency wallet will help in ensuring the safety of your capital. These crypto wallets are just like any other account you would have at a regular bank. Depending on the level of safety and security you need, there are different wallets available. Some of these are just like any of the regular wallets you use, and others are software or online-based wallets. You can download a wallet (either uses an online or offline one), select the method of storage (online or external device), or just write the private key on a paper and store the paper carefully. Make sure that you do plenty of research before you select a particular wallet.

Exchanges

An exchange is a third-party website that helps in bringing together buyers and sellers of cryptocurrencies located all over the world. There are various exchanges to choose from depending on the type of currency, the method of payment, and any applicable fees. Once you have created your account on an exchange, you will need to link your bank account and then make the necessary arrangements for moving these funds between these two accounts. There are various exchanges to choose from depending on your geographic location.

One-on-one meeting

If anonymity is paramount for you and going through all the steps in the methods mentioned above seem tiring to you, then in such a case, this option is for you. You can meet sellers or interested buyers of cryptocurrencies in your locality and trade directly with them. If you are living in a big city, this becomes quite easy and convenient. You can search for cryptocurrency sellers online, contact them, and then set up a meeting. Make sure that whenever you are meeting a seller, you are doing so in a public set up and aren't carrying a lot of currency with you.

Mining

The next method by which you can own digitized tokens of your choice is by mining them. You need a dedicated computer and the necessary software to start mining your cryptocurrency. There are specific mining specific devices that you might have to invest in initially, and the initial cost of investment might be high. If you don't want to start your mine, then you have the option of joining a mining pool and working along with other miners. The other option available to you is to start investing in other miners.

Whenever a block of transactions is successfully mined, everyone gets a share of the reward.

Investment trust

If you aren't too comfortable with the idea of buying and then storing large amounts of cryptocurrency, then you can start investing in any of the cryptocurrency investment funds. These trust funds are quite similar to any of the other regular investment funds. There will be an investment fund manager who does all the work for you, and all that you need to do is just provide the necessary capital

ATMs

It is a new concept and is quite similar to a face-to-face exchange, but it involves a teller machine. You will have to insert your currency or scan the QR code of your wallet, and you will receive the necessary codes for loading cryptocurrency into your online or hardware wallet. Exchange rates can differ, and you should check the necessary details beforehand.

Chapter Four: What is Blockchain Technology?

The overall look of the blockchain might seem quite similar to any of the Wikipedia pages you regularly visit. When it comes to a blockchain, people have the power of making entries into a record of information, and the network itself is controlled by a community of users. The users of the technology help in keeping it updated. This feature is quite similar to Wikipedia pages wherein there isn't a single publisher, and a separate entity doesn't control all the information available. Well, that's where the similarities between Wikipedia and blockchain end. The blockchain technology is unique; the Internet powers both these technologies.

Wikipedia is built into WWW by utilizing a client-server network model. On Wikipedia, any client who has the necessary authorizations has the power of changing any of the entries that are stored on the central server. Whenever a user is accessing a Wikipedia page, they will automatically receive an updated master copy of the concerned entry. Control of the database solely rests in the hands of the administrators at Wikipedia, and they are responsible for granting access and permissions.

The digital skeletons of Wikipedia are similar to the centralized and secure databases, which governments and banks make use of today. The control of the database rests with a centralized authority like the owners, and they have the power to decide who gets to access it and who doesn't. However, when it comes to the blockchain technology, its digital skeleton is entirely different. The master copy of Wikipedia can be edited on one server, and all of the users will now be able to see the edited version. In the case of the blockchain, every single node on the network tends to come to the same conclusion, and each carries on with updating the record independently. In such a case, the most famous recording automatically becomes the de-facto master copy.

Once this is done, the transactions are broadcasted, and every node creates their version of the updated events. It is this fundamental difference that makes the blockchain technology so much more useful and powerful. The blockchain represents innovation in the manner in which information is registered and distributed on the network, and it eliminates the need for a third-party.

The blockchain is an amalgamation of a couple of existing technologies for creating a different technique. The three parts of the blockchain are the Internet, the private key, and a protocol that governs the rewarding scheme. All this resulted in the creation of a digital system wherein interactions, and transactions could take place without the involvement of a third party. The manner in which the digital relationships are secured is quite elegant in its simplicity. The blockchain technology helps in redefining the concept of digital trust. Trust is the judgment of risk that exists between two parties. In the digitized world, it primarily relates to two important ideas and these are authentication and authorization. To simply put it, two fundamental questions need to be confirmed before a transaction is authorized and these are:

- *Are you who you say you are?*

- *Are you authorized to do what you are doing?*

When it comes to the blockchain technology, the private key helps in signifying the ownership and helps in authentication of transactions. The blockchain consists of huge blocks of data, which record and verify all the operations that take place/took place. The network is fully aware of every coin ever produced, and every coin can be accounted for as well. The blockchain is a public ledger with a record of all transactions that took place in the past, are taking place currently, and the ones that will take place in the future as well. It is akin to any bookkeeping tool you might have used.

When it comes to Bitcoin network, bookkeeping isn't a confidential process, and the information is available to the public. It doesn't mean that private details of an individual would be divulged. The blockchain keeps track of all the transactions, and these are just recorded in the form of wallet addresses. The identities of the owners are secure and aren't made public. It helps in maintaining security while improving transparency. Every computer on the network is referred to as a node and is running a wallet application that will help in detecting and validating every transaction that involves Bitcoins. Every node has a copy of the entire transactional history of Bitcoin transactions. The blockchain grows when a new block of Bitcoins is added to it after it been verified by the nodes. These new blocks are simply added to the existing ones and contain the summary of the previous block. Once a block has been added to this chain, it cannot be changed or altered.

On the blockchain, a transaction is entered into the public record only after it has been verified. Once a transaction becomes a part of the network, it cannot be deleted or altered ever again. The blockchain consists of huge blocks of data, and every block of data that is mined produces a hash. A hash is similar to the summary of a block. No one can determine the sequence of a hash before it has been produced and therefore, no one can tamper with it. Apart from this, every block of data consists the hash of the previous block as well. It means that no one has the power of altering one block of information without compromising the integrity of the entire network.

Chapter Five: Best Cryptocurrencies

Ethereum

Ethereum is indeed a real outlier. The platform that Ethereum makes use of provides the network with a framework to execute smart contracts that are powered by a decentralized network. The team of digital wizards who are responsible for managing Ethereum is extremely good at what they do. It is not just the team, but also the degree of adoption it has that makes Ethereum quite phenomenal. A developer can use this network for running distributed applications or Dapps. Ethereum is a peer-to-peer network. It doesn't matter what these computer programs are made up of and the network is optimized in such a way that it will carry out all the rules and execute the standards in an almost mechanical manner as soon as a couple of conditions have been met, just like the execution of a contract. Ethereum has a decentralized blockchain, and it is a public network that collectively helps in storing data in a cryptographic format, enables the execution of contracts, and even lends a layer of security to its functioning. Every computer or node on this network has to download a small virtual machine that is used for syncing various contracts.

This system is very diverse, and it helps in providing security, safety, reliability, and convenience to all the users.

This system isn't free or even private, so designers simply use it for acquiring agreement on results and when the information is openly accessible. It doesn't work the way computerized cash or installment framework would and it instead plans to give "fuel" that will help in the working of the Dapps or decentralized applications on the system. It may sound somewhat muddled, yet it isn't. Think about this as a decentralized online journal and for erasing, posting, or adjusting a note; you will be required to pay an exchange expense as Ether for making the required changes or for its execution.

Bitcoin

A standout amongst the most well-known digital forms of currency today is Bitcoin. In fact, Bitcoin pioneered the cryptocurrency revolution. In the course of the most recent few years, this currency has positively demonstrated its worth. A Bitcoin is worth more than an ounce of gold as of now, and its market price seems to be growing steadily. It makes use of the blockchain for securing the exchanges and different transactions on the network while lending anonymity to its users. The Bitcoin was the first cryptocurrency that made use of the blockchain technology for processing and storing information on the system.

Litecoin

Litecoin was presented to the world by Charles Lee who is a former Google employee as the "silver" to the "gold" of Bitcoin. Lee had thought of the possibility of Litecoin to settle the issues that Bitcoins suffered from. Litecoin, similar to alternate cryptographic forms of money, isn't issued by an administration. The governments have been responsible for the circulation and the printing of fiat currency along with the central banks and other regulatory authorities. Litecoins aren't controlled by the Federal Reserve, and they aren't stamped at a press at the Bureau of Engraving and Printing. Litecoins are preferably made by a perplexing procedure alluded to as mining. This process involves the recording and verification of all the transactions that take place on the network. There can be close to 84 million Litecoins available at any given point in time, and unlike fiat currency, this amount cannot be exceeded.

Auroracoin

Auroracoin was invented in 2014 amidst a background of a failing economy and financial chaos that hit Iceland back in 2008. It was created for solving the currency crisis that Iceland was facing when it became the victim of ambiguity and high expectations that people were harboring about the government's role in the crisis.

During 2008-09, Iceland was rocked by a severe financial crisis. Most of the banks in Iceland collapsed, and thousands of citizens lost all their savings. All this pushed Iceland into a high debt, and it resulted in more than 1/4th of all the homeowners defaulting on their payments for mortgages. The banking system grew fragile, and the Krona was devalued. These circumstances led to the collapse of the government in Iceland, and the citizens were keen on developing a financial system that was free from all this mess. The Auroracoin was created for cleaning up this mess, and it was created on the principles of decentralization. The Auroracoin, like any other cryptocurrency, was free from the restraints of the regular banking system. Even this coin has a fixed supply, and the forces of demand and supply govern its prices. Auroracoin made a comeback in 2015, and its prices have been steadily increasing since then.

Emercoin

The Emercoin or Emer is based on a decentralized blockchain like Bitcoins and is used for the immediate settlement of transactions. It relies on peer-to-peer technology, and it doesn't need a central authority to monitor its functioning. The consensus on the network helps in the verification and the confirmation of the transactions that take place on the system. Emer combines its code with a portion of codes from Bitcoin, Peercoin, and Namecoin. The Emercoin is one of the favorite Altcoins in the market today, and it facilitates its users in the exchange of money and information from anywhere in the world at any given point in time. Just like any other cryptocurrency, you need to have private keys for authorizing a transaction using Emer. Emercoin was developed by a team of Russian developers. The group consisted of eight experts in the field of cryptocurrency, technology, and finance. It makes use of proof-of-stake principal for mining along with Proof-of-work principle. The limit on this currency is quite dynamic.

Chapter Six: Tips for Trading

Cryptocurrencies are referred to virtual currencies as well, and their share in the global financial economy is rapidly growing. At present, there are more than 800 cryptocurrencies in the market. Investing in cryptos isn't an exact science. Unlike a company that trades its shares publicly, there aren't any financial statements to go through and therefore it is impossible to calculate the book value of cryptocurrencies. Since the intrinsic value of cryptos isn't known, it is difficult to determine their actual worth.

A simple trading fact is that you will never be able to time your buys or sells correctly in the crypto market. There isn't one single strategy that you can follow for acquiring more wealth since selling isn't an exact science. Not only does every trader have different goals, but all cryptocurrencies are different as well. In this section, you will learn about some tips that you can make use of while investing in cryptocurrencies.

Understanding the power of cryptocurrencies

It is a general misconception that investing in cryptocurrencies is the same as investing in stocks. Well, cryptocurrencies aren't stocks, and they indeed aren't commodities. Cryptocurrencies and stocks both have prices but are both fundamentally different. The process of exchange might be quite similar. The underlying technology that powers cryptos have the potential to be adapted for retail and institutional capital. The decentralized nature of digitized currencies means that there isn't much scope for any manipulation. Invest because you want to and not because everyone else seems to be doing the same.

Select a strategy

How often do you want to trade? Do you want to be a day trader, or do you want to hold on to your digitized tokens for a while longer? The general rule of thumb is that the longer you hold; the lesser is the risk that you can incur. It is one rule of investing that applies to stocks and cryptocurrencies as well. However, it doesn't mean that when the circumstances aren't favorable, you hold on to the digitized tokens. Learn to cut your losses and exit, whenever you feel like you are incurring a loss.

The initial investment

You can effectively reduce the risk of any sudden changes by dollar cost averaging your purchases of any cryptos.

Doing this will help in reducing the prick of any sudden price fluctuations in the market. Stick to your gut when it comes to investing, but it doesn't mean that you simply ignore the market trends.

Hedging your bets

Plenty of exchanges allow you to short order as well. It enables you to place a bet on either side of the price movements of your crypto. For instance, a simple strategy would be to put 90% on long orders and the rest on short orders. An approach like this one means that you are confident about the extended position and it can be made use of for any level of risk.

Trading in altcoins

Bitcoins and other famous cryptos are quite tempting. However, the world of digitized currencies certainly isn't restricted to just the popular cryptos. So, don't ignore other altcoins because the smaller market capitalization they offer means that they are prone to higher movements in their price. Different altcoins are created for catering to the needs of different niches. The risk of investing in altcoins might seem high, but then the returns are equally good. You can allocate specific percentages to different altcoins depending on your tolerance of risk. It is quite similar to managing a fund. Some altcoins are more stable than Ethereum, but others can be very volatile. So, a significant chunk of your portfolio can consist of the famous cryptocurrencies, and the rest can be made up of other altcoins.

Get into the game

Bitcoins are at an all-time high, and the returns they are offering are mind-boggling. It is not just the Bitcoins that are performing incredibly well; all other cryptos are doing well too. All the tips and information you have gathered so far will be of no use if you don't get into the game. You should get started with investing. After all, gaining experience is the best way to learn. Start with a small investment, and you can slowly progress towards more significant investments.

Separate wallets

Never make use of one wallet for storing all your digital tokens. By making use of one wallet for spending and saving your cryptocurrencies, you are making yourself vulnerable to cyber threats and attacks. You can create as many Bitcoin addresses as you want. So, it makes sense to make use of different wallets for this purpose. Use different addresses for storing, sending, and receiving cryptocurrencies.

Web wallets shouldn't be used for safekeeping

Web wallets are easy to use. However, it doesn't necessarily mean that they are secure as well. In fact, you are making yourself a soft target for all the hackers. If someone manages to hack into your web wallet, you might as well forget about your precious coins. You can make use of a web wallet for holding onto small savings and quick transactions, but that's about it. Always store your savings on a hardware wallet that isn't online. Cryptos don't work for your credit or debit cards. Once your card gets stolen, you lose it or even forget the password; you have the option of blocking and receiving a new one. However, you cannot do this with cryptocurrencies. Since the network is based on anonymity and it is decentralized, there isn't a regulatory authority that you can report the theft too, and you are bound to lose your coins. So, be careful with your tokens.

Protecting your privacy

You are the only one who is responsible for your security and no one else. You wouldn't share the PIN of your bank account with others, would you? Similarly, you shouldn't share your private key with anyone else. The wallet address you use is like your bank account, and your key is like the PIN. The private key is necessary for officiating a transaction. Anyone who is in possession of your private key and the wallet address can easily siphon the funds from your account. Let us keep all the technical aspects aside for a moment. Isn't it foolish to divulge your private information to a stranger?

Cold storage

You are vulnerable, even if your cryptocurrency is stored in a wallet on your computer. Applications of different purses tend to store user data, and its location can be predicted easily. It is a severe breach of security if someone can access all your financial information. A simple solution is to store your private key on an offline media. Ensuring additional safety will do you no harm, and it will help in securing your hard-earned money. You have the option of printing the private key on a piece of paper or even store it on a USB. You can scan your QR code and save it. Another option is the encryption of your key. Without the code to decrypt it, the numbers of the key would be useless.

Never invest more than you can afford to lose

When it comes to investing in any form of security, it is essential that you spend wisely. You should never invest more than the loss you can afford. Cryptos are volatile and speculative. The chances of earning a profit or incurring a loss are equally high. So, if you are taking a risk, make sure that it is a calculated one and not an impulsive one. One poor decision can lead to a significant loss. You should be comfortable with the investment that you are making. Always prepare for the worst, you never know what might happen to your investment. You might even end up losing everything. Also, try and diversify your portfolio so that you don't miss everything due to the volatility of a single cryptocurrency.

Set goals for every trade you make

It is quintessential that you have set goals for every deal that you think of making. It will help in keeping a steady mind even when the market conditions aren't favorable. Set a price limit at which you should take profits and cut your losses. Set these two limits before you think about entering the market. This will help you in staying level headed without getting swayed by emotions.

Technology

If you are thinking about investing in a programmable currency that you will need a basic understanding of the underly8ing technology. Most of the cryptocurrencies make use of the same code as that of a Bitcoin and are just pale copies of the former. Therefore, the investor tends to take little interest in it, unless the Bitcoin fails, as another cryptocurrency can act as its substitute. Take into consideration the validation system that the blockchain makes use of. Does the cryptocurrency make the method of proof of work or evidence of stake? Both are being used simultaneously, or neither is being used? Does it use any other algorithm for checking the transactions on the blockchain? What's the governance that's involved, if any? What method of scalability is considered? Is the cryptocurrency even making use of a blockchain? Cryptocurrencies that don't possess the same characteristics like the Bitcoin or which doesn't use the same language for programming should be studied carefully. Don't assume that all the cryptocurrencies are the same.

The number of tokens created

As an investor, you will be buying tokens, so you should check if the cryptocurrency has a finite number of coins and if the system is deflationary. The quantum of coins in existence can increase or decrease the price of the cryptocurrency at any point in time. For instance, Bitcoin and Bitcoin cash can only have 21 million tokens at any point in time. So, this is a scarce resource, and with an increase in their demand, their value is bound to increase as well.

The price of a token

Finding a virtual currency that seems to be promising isn't sufficient, you should also know when to buy it. A cryptocurrency can be purchased before its official launch by participating in an ICO or Initial Coin Offering. However, you need to take into consideration the fact that the price of the currency can drop significantly after the brief high of an ICO. If you have missed the ICO, then don't worry. Just wait till the public attention fades away. The price of a cryptocurrency is bound to increase when it is added to an existing trading platform, is taken up by a popular wallet service, or when it has reached the stage of track record. It is wise to buy these tokens before the happening of any of these events when the price isn't too high, and you still have a safety margin working in your favor. There are different trading platforms, websites, and exchanges that will provide you with the necessary charts for judging the performance of a cryptocurrency.

Website matters

Check whether the cryptocurrency you want to invest in has an official website of its own. Is there any information available about its creators or the company that's running the operations? Are there any developers and if yes, then their biographies and any white papers describing the nature of the cryptocurrency in question? If you cannot find all this information, then it is better if you stay away from such currency. What if it turns out to be a Ponzi scam? Don't invest blindly.

Slack

Slack is the communication platform used by most of the cryptocurrency developers. By registering yourself on slack, you can obtain all the necessary information about the performance of the cryptocurrencies and any advancement made in this regard. Always take into consideration the developers who are responsible for the creation of a particular token. So, do plenty of research, read about the team, and acquire all the information needed, and only then should you make a decision about investing. Being prudent is quintessential.

Mistakes to avoid

There are a couple of errors that you should avoid if you want to invest in cryptocurrencies successfully. The first thing that you should do is store your crypto offline. Security should be your priority, and you should always secure your digitized currencies. Once they are lost, they cannot be recovered. Take precautions while storing your cryptos and store them offline. Don't forget that if you don't have your private key, you cannot access your coins. Do not get carried away by any pump and dump groups. Don't follow these teams and don't think of a quick buy. Instead, do your research and invest in coins sensibly. When in doubt, invest in the popular coins before you think about the obscure ones.

Most people tend to buy or spend in certain cryptos because they are considered to be a hot investment at present. However, don't do this. Investing in a crypto that you know nothing about will do you no good. So, take some time and do plenty of research before jumping into the market. Who wouldn't want to make a quick buck? ICOs tend to promote this, but that doesn't mean they are an excellent investing option. Like with any other form of investment, you should do plenty of research on your own before investing in an ICO. After all, it is your hard-earned money that you are thinking about investing. So, that is the least you can do. Don't panic and sell your position. You will end up regretting it. Don't let your emotions guide you when you are engaging in a trade. Be practical and only take calculated risks. Never seek advice from a stranger. Do your research and trust your channels. Make a decision just after gaining a thorough understanding of the crypto you have opted for.

Strategies for Risk Minimization

Investing is risky in general and investing in cryptocurrencies is a high-risk, high return activity. At present, there is no other category of investment that has potential as high as the one offered by cryptocurrencies. However, with high rewards, the risk involved is quite high too. As a crypto investor, there are a couple of risks that you should be aware of.

Cryptocurrencies and all kinds of digital tokens are considered to be extremely volatile. The volatility of Bitcoins has relatively reduced over the years, but all the other forms of cryptocurrencies experience intra-day price movements that can move in either of the directions. The market for cryptocurrencies is news-driven, and every crypto has its risk, rumors, sensationalized headlines, and spiteful media campaigns by the rival blockchain technologies can result in significant price drops and unfavorable fluctuations in the value of the cryptocurrencies. As an investor, you can significantly reduce your market risk by diversifying your investment portfolio. Your portfolio of cryptocurrencies shouldn't consist of just one form of crypto and should have smallholdings of other altcoins as well. You can further reduce your market risk by hedging your investment portfolio with BTC futures as well.

Another challenge that investors who are investing in mid-cap and small-cap coins are the risk of liquidity. At present, the average trading volume of Bitcoin per day is over $2 billion. If you leave the ten largest cryptos according to their market share, investors are left with a trading volume that's less than $100 million daily, and in most of the cases, it is less than $10 million. Anyone who is looking to make a more significant investment will find this situation quite challenging. Not just that, the trading volumes of the cryptos are spread over different exchanges, and it makes it quite tricky for executing a large order. For mitigating the risk posed by liquidity, try sticking to those cryptos that are quite liquid, especially when you are trading in large volumes.

Cryptocurrencies are a decentralized form of currencies. However, regulatory uncertainty poses to be a significant hurdle for any seller. Whenever a considerable cryptocurrency trading platform announces any adverse cryptocurrency norms, the entire market gets shaken.

For instance, China had recently proclaimed a ban on ICOs (initial coin offerings), and this caused a significant drop in the prices of Chinese digital currencies like NEO.

Regulatory risk isn't just confined to one region of the world. All those who are investing in cryptocurrencies should follow any legal news about the tokens they are investing in quite regularly. At present, the major governments of the world haven't banned the use of cryptocurrencies. However, if they do so, then the effect can be devastating. Sadly, regulatory risk cannot be mitigated, and all that an investor can do is follow the news closely and act accordingly.

When it comes to trading cryptocurrencies and storing funds, operational risks are bound to exist. The major centralized Bitcoin exchanges happen to be frequent targets for cybercriminals. Even if you are making use of own wallets for storing your funds, you might still suffer a loss if you don't store your holdings in cold storage. If you are interested in minimizing the operational risk you face, then you should make use of decentralized exchanges and opt for hardware wallets while storing your funds.

Regardless of what you would like to believe, if you are investing in cryptocurrencies, you are a target for hackers. Most of the digitized currencies are pseudonymous, and this makes them an ideal target for cybercriminals out there. Unfortunately, the crypto space is filled with fake websites, fraudulent email campaigns, and targeted hacking of vulnerable trading platforms. A significant risk that crypto investors should be varied of is cybercrime. There are no generalized tips for mitigating this risk, and as an investor, you should take all the necessary steps for ensuring the cyber-safety of your investments and holdings.

Numerous schemes promise unrealistically high returns and are often promoted across different social media platforms and at times are even advertised on reputable cryptocurrency media outlets. Usually, these are just pyramid schemes. However, scammers keep coming up with fraudulent ICOs for scamming novice investors. Prudence and research can prevent you from falling prey to such scams. Make sure that you are doing your research and aren't investing because someone asked or told you to.

Well, it might seem like there are plenty of risks that you might have to face as an investor, but you can successfully mitigate your chances by taking a couple of simple steps. Make sure that you keep these risks in mind before entering the cryptocurrency market.

Conclusion

I would like to thank you for purchasing this book.

If you are interested in investing in cryptocurrencies, then the first thing that you should be focusing on is doing research. The decisions you make should be based on the information you have gathered. After all, it is your money, and you should make sure that the investment you have decided to make is definitely worth your while. So, always make it a point to check the history, future and the current trade practices of different digitized currencies before you think about making any decisions.

Remember that you don't necessarily have to invest in only the popular cryptocurrencies because everyone around you is. Bitcoins are famous, and everyone wants to jump on the bandwagon. However, all the excessive demand might signify exorbitant prices. There are plenty of other cryptocurrencies to choose from that are equally good. There are several exchanges and platforms that you can make use of depending on your investment needs.

Thank you and all the best.

Thank You

Once again thank you for taking the time to invest in **The Science of Cryptocurrencies**. If this book has impacted you in anyway. Feel free to leave an honest review on Amazon at:-

http://www.amazon.com/gp/product-review/B078XSLXXL

After leaving your review feel free to contact me at quawsisamuel@gmail.com to receive a **special offer.**

Bonus!

Wouldn't it be nice to have essential information for investing in Cryptocurrencies, forex, commodities ,stocks and options for Free. Well now is your Chance !!

Enter into web browser-

http://eepurl.com/dgGQ5v

Simply click the above link to obtain a free promotional item. I would also give you full exclusive access to our service which I give relevant information, tips and strategic notification on a variety of investments markets and concepts that will help boost your returns on investment.

Resources

https://investinghaven.com/reading-markets/10-investment-tips-cryptocurrencies-investing/

https://blockgeeks.com/guides/what-is-cryptocurrency/

https://blockgeeks.com/guides/what-is-blockchain-technology/

https://www.coindesk.com/information/what-is-blockchain-technology/

http://en.auroracoin.is

Made in the USA
Coppell, TX
03 June 2020

26903370R00039